5 Lessons for Liat

A coming of age book of poems looking into an unknowingly free spirited child, Liat.

Fiza Akram

BookLeaf
Publishing

Presentation by *BookLeaf Publishing*

Web: www.bookleafpub.com

E-mail: info@bookleafpub.com

ISBN: 978-93-95890-50-2

First edition 2022

*To my family and friends who have always been
there for me, especially in the
last 3 years. I appreciate you all so much.*

Let the clay melt away

God sent Liat an angel,
so the light inside Liat's heart could reach
the surface of her skin.
Liat lived alone in her castle unaware of
God's plan.
God sent Liat an angel,
so the simple gratitude and joy around her
could be witnessed within her, to the brim.

The walls of her castle were made of clay,
but the angel knew its way.
God sent Liat an angel,
So the walls of clay could melt away.

Liat resisted the angel and built more walls
of clay,
but the angel persisted.
God sent Liat an angel,
so the walls of clay could be melted away
with the sunshine and the rain.

Liat was drawn to the sunshine,
she melted away the walls of clay and found
a home under the angel's wing.
God sent Liat an angel,
so she could let people inside her life and be
more than just fine.

We are just fine

God sent Liat an angel,
so the angel could give her care
'Oh how fleeting time is' Liat would
exclaim in despair.
God sent Liat an angel,
so Liat could read time not with her watch
but with the angel's steady ticking heartbeat.

Liat looked out her rose tinted window
everyday,
she hoped to freeze time someday.
God sent Liat an angel,
So she could enjoy the pink hue everyday.

Liat looked out the window to see a crab
retreating into the ocean one evening.
Oh how she wished she knew where to go
like the crab.
God sent Liat an angel,
so she could enjoy the present moment at
bay before the waves took her away.

The waves took her

away

When the storm arrived and turbulent waves
took her away from shore,
Liat searched for the angel,
it was what she wanted at core.
God sent Liat an angel,
so the angel could give her more.

As winter grew stronger and the night grew
longer,
Liat had to put up a fight.
Sometimes the angel wasn't in sight in the
pitch dark night,
but she thought his light was enough for her
to keep going for the night.
Little did she know, it was her own inner
light and might.

As the storm calmed down,
Liat found the crown of bravery, its jewels
became her light.
It was time for her to go back to her castle's
armoury, and lay down her weapons.
She hoped this was the end of her misery.
God sent Liat an angel,

Not to tuck her into bed, but to make her
realize she was capable of giving her inner
child a peaceful night's sleep instead.

Peaceful night's sleep

All Liat wanted was a peaceful night's sleep,
however, God had other plans.
God sent Liat an angel,
but it was time for the angel to leave.

Liat cried, screamed and grieved but the
angel was determined to leave.
The angel's wings disappeared into the same
light it came from.
There was only a boyish devil in sight.
Was this Liats angel?

Oh, how she was caught in a storm again.
The rain seemed unbearable,
until she looked at the puddle under her feet.
Liat saw a reflection of herself,
Looking radiant and elite.
She felt a tingling sensation on her back.
She had grown a pair of wings,
much bigger than the ones the angel had.
God sent Liat an angel,
so she could inherit all the good the angel
once had.

What the angel once had

Liat re-built her walls of clay.
Each day she laid a brick made of clay.
She knew they would melt away some day.
She wasn't building the walls for them to
stay forever.
Liat built herself a home, where her wings
could rest before the next endeavour.

Her wings wiped the sweat off her forehead,
and they gave her shade.
She wore them with pride because they
displayed her pure inner light.

Liat built her walls of clay each day.
The task was challenging with every passing
day.
However, she wasn't alone at bay.

Overtime she built her walls.
The corridors were empty, but the beauty
was not hidden for long.
One autumn morning there was a knock at
her door.

It was time for her to stretch her wings,
and take on her next endeavour.

God sent an angel,
This time her name was Liat.